RAIL 5 PORTFOLIOS

The 37s

Compiled by
Howard Johnston

Copyright © Jane's Publishing Company Limited 1986

First published in the United Kingdom in 1986 by
Jane's Publishing Company Limited
238 City Road, London EC1V 2PU

ISBN 0 7106 0363 0

Typeset by Netherwood Dalton & Co Ltd, Huddersfield

Printed by Netherwood Dalton & Co Ltd, Huddersfield

JANE'S

Cover illustrations

Front: Having berthed their train of loaded clay hoods, Nos 37247
and 37181 await departure from Carne Point with empties bound for
St Blazey. Both locomotives are sporting local embellishments,
No 37181 with the happy Cornish lizzard while No 37247 simply
proclaims its ownership as 'Cornish Railways'. *(Hugh Dady)*
Nikkormat FT2 50mm Nikkor Kodachrome 64 1/250, f5.6

Rear: Then designated English Electric Type 3, Stratford-based No
D6711 emerges from Peascliffe Tunnel on the East Coast Main Line
with a nearly empty southbound rake of Carflats on 28 May 1966.
(Michael Mensing)
Nikkorex F 50mm Nikkor Agfa CT18 1/500, f3.5

This page: This is a book where there is no need to reflect on past
glories... the best is yet to come. 37260 is a fine example, and two
anonymous decades working out of Eastern Region depots have been
replaced by a new career in the Far North of Scotland which in 1984
saw it selected as the testbed for revolutionary radio signalling cab
equipment – hence the name *Radio Highland* unveiled at Dingwall
station prior to a run to Kyle of Lochalsh on 7 July 1984. In quieter
mood, 37260 stands in the sunshine at Stratford depot on 11 July
1981. *(Hugh Dady)*
Praktica IV 50mm Tessar Kodachrome 64 1/200, f7

Introduction

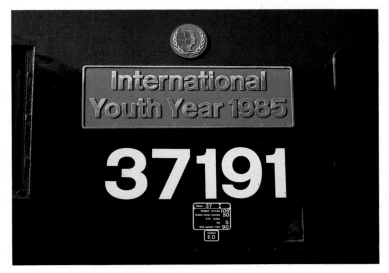

In the total absence of a Class 37 Preservation Society (we don't need one), this book is intended as an appreciation of British Rail's born-again locomotive type.

It's reassuring to know that not quite everything we hold dear will be swept away in the name of progress as BR plans its motive power fleet to take us into the 21st Century.

The 1750hp English Electric Type 3s weren't much to get excited about when they first came on the scene 25 years ago, but like roses, they do grow on you. D6700's debut on the Eastern Region in drab all-over green livery back in 1960 made little impact on the railway scene, and the dismay spread to the North-East, South Wales and Scottish Lowlands as within five years no fewer than 309 standardised examples had supplanted steam types. A general decline in traffic in recent times has seen their work extended to the South-West, across the Midlands, and West Highland and Far North outposts of the Scottish Region.

Why have the 37s survived where other designs failed? Perhaps it is because they are simply another stage in a well-tried design dating back to well before the Second World War. Now the familiar "dognose" bodyshell is being reappraised and renovated for an extended life at least until the year 2005.

To us all, the EE Type 3s are true mixed-traffic locos, at home with the duties performed before them in steam days by the GWR's 2-8-0s and 'Hall' and 'Grange' 4-6-0s, LNER B1s, Q6s and WDs, LMS Black 5s, and BR Standard types.

There were always minor technical differences between the first batch of 119 locos and the rest, but there again BR never was an organisation for total conformity. From 1985 there will be many more, as separate fleets are created to cash in on passenger and freight opportunities. New liveries, new numbers, and new pastures for many old friends. As for dear old split-headcode D6700, it will enter the 1990s with a face lifted front end, and doubtless a place in the hearts of the next generation of rail enthusiasts.

A short-lived naming was that of 37191, whose *International Youth Year 1985* plates were attached at Glasgow Queen Street on 21 January, and removed without ceremony at Eastfield on 15 November of the same year. *(Tom Noble)*
Mamiya 645   Ektachrome 200

Some of the country's finest photographers have loaned material from their collections for this book. Our thanks go to them.

HOWARD JOHNSTON
Huntingdon
November 1985

Opposite. In the beginning there was Liverpool Street... This former Great Eastern terminus was the starting point of the Class 37 invasion of BR tracks back in December 1960 with the arrival of D6700 at Stratford. Only now are they becoming a rare sight, supplanted first by more powerful Sulzer Class 47s and now by electric locos that are common user with the London Midland's West Coast Main Line. This is 37082 (since refurbished as 37502 for Railfreight), about to set off on the time-honoured Norwich run on 6 May 1978. *(Gavin Morrison)*
Pentax SP1000   Kodachrome 25

Right. To many this is the Class 37 at its all-time best, a smart Brunswick green with the colourful touch of yellow on the front end. D6814, pictured here at March on 19 May 1963, was one of the final series fitted with nose-end doors and split headcode boxes. New to Tinsley in early 1963, it was always an Eastern passenger loco until the great 1980s switch-round. Transformed with a new livery after leaving for Scotland in early 1981, and 37114 has now gained fame after christening as *Dunrobin Castle* for the 1985 reopening of the station of the same name. Like all boilered 37s however, it should eventually become part of the Railfreight fleet. (*John Feild*)
Kodak Retinette Agfa CT18 1/250, f4

Left. Lack of need for nose-end doors enabled English Electric to tidy up the design from D6819 onwards, and repositioning of the four-character headcode into one central panel made for a more stylish machine than hitherto... until work stained the green paint and safety rules dictated a less than glamorous full yellow end. This is D6975 between D6974 and a Class 86 electric at Doncaster Works during acceptance tests on 4 April 1965 before delivery to the WR. Now 37275, this loco has spent its entire career working from Cardiff Canton depot. (*John Feild*)
Kodak Retinette Agfa CT18 1/250, f5.6

The first couple of dozen English Electric Type 3s were delivered from late 1962 onwards in a drab livery of uninterrupted green decorated with the familiar half-size yellow warning panel across the front ends. D6722, still in original condition, approaches Chelmsford on 8 June 1962 with the 1045 Norwich-Liverpool Street. The overhead wires were energised but not yet ready for public services. By 1985 this Great Eastern loco had migrated to Scotland, and Eastfield depot had applied a much more enlightened livery with a profusion of blue, yellow and white. *(Michael Mensing)* *Hasselblad 1000F   Tessar f2.8 80mm* *High Speed Ektachrome   1/1000, f4*

The nose-end doors were so rarely used during multiple working that it was decided to dispense with them altogether after the emergence of D6818 from Vulcan Foundry in March 1963. These two views show the loco in two liveries.

Above. D6818 in green livery at Norwich on 9 November 1968 prior to taking out the 1800 Norwich-Cambridge service. Although new to Tinsley, it had migrated to Stratford by this date. *(Colin Ding)*
Rolleiflex
80mm Planar
High Speed Ektachrome
1/500, f5.6

Below. Renumbered 37118, the same loco stands in March East Yard on 15 June 1976 awaiting the signal for departure with a special Harwich-Glasgow Speedlink demonstration train. The headcode blinds, isolated six months earlier, have been specially revived for the occasion.
(Howard Johnston)
Praktica LB2   50mm
Ektachrome 64   1/125, f8

Opposite. A rare shot of a green Class 37 on green Southern Region stock, and on the now closed Great Central's London Extension at that! The 1008 York-Bournemouth West speeds through Wolfhampcote and over the Oxford Canal south of the site of Braunston and Willoughby station on 18 April 1964 with D6801 at the head. The line closed a little over two years later, while the loco, now 37101, was in 1985 unusual in never having strayed from the Eastern Region. *(Michael Mensing)*
Nikkorex F   Nikkor
50mm   Agfacolor CT18
1/500, f3.5

Electric traction was due to take over most workings on the Harwich branch from May 1986, but that did not mean the end of the 37s – just a transfer away to other duties. This is 37049, a 1962 loco whose modest allocation history in its first 20 years was Tinsley, Ipswich, Stratford, Healey Mills and March before the call to Scotland came in mid-1985. This shot shows the ecs from the up boat train being led into Parkeston Yard on 14 April 1984. *(Gavin Morrison)*
Pentax SP1000   Kodachrome 25   1/250, f4.5

Although from a different stable, the Brush-built Class 31 has had a lot in common with the Class 37 since it was rebuilt with the same English Electric power unit, albeit set at a lower rating, from the mid-1960s onwards, and this view of the morning Mile End sand train leaving Marks Tey yard on 19 September 1983 demonstrates how compatible they really are. Leading loco is 37173 (which incidentally turns up at Liverpool on p54), with 31412 behind. Marks Tey, on the GE main line out of Liverpool Street, forms the junction for the truncated Cambridge line to Sudbury.
(Gordon T Bird)
Canon AE1   28mm Tamron
Kodachrome 64   1/250, f4-5.6

Left. This 24 July 1980 view of the 1600 King's Lynn-Liverpool Street shows 37047 in its final phase as a passenger loco. Railfreight now calls the tune because 37047's boiler has been isolated pending removal at Crewe Works during the overhaul that should see it emerge with a new livery and a new identity. The location is Downham Market, a Great Eastern location practically unchanged in the best part of a century. *(Hugh Ballantyne)*
Leica M3   50mm Summicron
Kodachrome 25   1/250, f4

Above. The superb early evening sunlight over an East Suffolk dockland shows off the finer points of one of the most familiar locos on the Great Eastern system. 37054, final member of the original series built with a steam-heat boiler, drifts into Lowestoft with a through train over the East Suffolk line from Liverpool Street on 24 July 1980. March depot clung on to 37054 for ten years, but that boiler is now no more. Since May 1984 through services from Liverpool Street to Lowestoft have been a thing of the past too. *(Hugh Ballantyne)*
Leica M3   50mm Summicron
Kodachrome 25   1/250, f2.8

Framed by the girders of the river bridge at Chesterton, just north of Cambridge, 37109 heads south with a Whitemoor-Temple Mills freight. The date is 1 June 1981 and the front end headcodes have been replaced by marker lights. Originally Tinsley passenger loco D6809, it had migrated to March by early 1974. (*Michael Rhodes*)

Canon AE1   100mm
Kodachrome 64   1/250, f5.6

Twenty-five years ago, the flat Fenland land-scape that was the GN and GE Joint Line between Spalding and March would resound to the endless procession of Thompson B1s, WD 2-8-0s and BR Standard 9Fs on coal traffic. It had fallen away so drastically when this view of the Doncaster-Middleton Towers sand train was taken on 25 November 1982 that the line had only two days to live. Thornaby's 37067 has left Cowbit and passes the home signal just north of Postland station. Now weeds mark the spot. (Paul Johnston)
Pentax ME Super   Ektachrome 64
1/250, f5.6

Below. At least there are a few old-stagers left on the Great Eastern! While many of their sisters have left the area for more glamorous work in Scotland and elsewhere, split head-code pair 37086 and 37102 were still around to double-head a Freightliner under the wires at Stratford on 28 September 1984. RSH Darlington-built 37086 has been a March loco since mid-1974, while Vulcan-built 37102 has had a similar Cambridgeshire pedigree. What future home for them after refurbishment, however? Certainly they will not be on this particular task for long, once the wires go up on the North London line. *(Ken Harris)*
Yashica TL Electro X   80mm Zeiss
Kodachrome 64   1/500, f4

Right. Modern Speedlink vehicles can make a really colourful sight, as this freight leaving March's Whitemoor Up Yard for Peterborough West Yard on 12 April 1985 demonstrates. Loco 37092 is maintained only a couple of hundred yards to the left of the picture, and has been since 1976. *(John Rudd)*
Mamiya 645   80mm Fujichrome 50
1/250, f5.6

Left. Class 37 deliveries to the WR began in March 1963, when the first of an order for 100 units (D6819-D6918) arrived at Cardiff Canton. Others followed and as elsewhere the locos soon acquitted themselves well. They have characterised the South Wales freight scene ever since. 37244 had become very shabby indeed by 10 June 1976 when this view of a down empty coal train through Newport was caught by the camera. This loco, built by Vulcan Foundry in 1964, has been slogging continuously on South Wales freights ever since, but the vacuum-braked vehicles have given way to more modern stock. This loco was one of the first handful to be dual-braked back in 1968.
(Hugh Ballantyne)
Leica M3
50mm Summicron
Kodachrome 25
1/250, f4-5.6

Right. A brilliantly sunny day enabled the perfect photography of 37186 on this train of coal empties down the long, straight slow line through Marshfield, between Newport and Cardiff, on 23 August 1978. The trend of plating over the front-end marker light panel was reversed in the mid-1980s by some of the more enterprising depots. Of all the South Wales 37s, this one is a passenger version. D6875-92 were built in 1963-64 with steamheater boilers, and several retain them to this day.
(Hugh Ballantyne)
Leica M3
50mm Summicron
Kodachrome 25
1/500, f3.5

Who could ever forget the sight of a triple-header? A 5000-plus horsepower threesome was rostered for the punishingly heavy iron ore trains from Port Talbot to Llanwern steelworks until the arrival of more powerful pairs of Class 56s saw them split up. Couplings had to be specially strengthened for 37307 + 37298 + 37305 to haul this typical loaded train into Llanwern on 15 April 1977. The first and last locos are now 37403 and 37407 respectively on Scotland's West Highland Line.
(Hugh Ballantyne)
Leica M3   50mm Summicron
Kodachrome 25   1/125, f4

The first visits of pairs of Class 37s to London via the GW main line was for high-speed trials with passenger stock back in 1965. They still make occasional appearances nowadays, although the absence of an allocation at Old Oak Common restricts their use to trains such as those to Foster Yeoman stone terminals. On 14 May 1982 37303 and 37288 speed down the main line near Twyford with empties for Merehead quarry. Unlike many of the later series of 37s, 37303 has been retained as a freight loco, while 37288 has been refurbished as 37427 for the Western Region.
(Rodney A Lissenden)
Pentax 6 × 7 Ektachrome 200 1/500, f8

Left. The reduction in coal business saw the Aber Junction (Caerphilly)-Taffs Well (Radyr) connection closed to its surviving freight traffic at the end of 1982. On 2 April of that year (to be remembered as the day of the Falklands Invasion), 37279 and 37288 join the former Taff Vale main line at Walnut Tree Junction with a southbound mgr. Both locos moved up to Scotland in 1985 prior to eth conversion as 37424 and 37427 respectively.
(Michael Mensing)
Bronica S2A   Nikkor 75mm
Agfachrome 50S   1/500, f8

Right. There is real scenic beauty in the Welsh Valleys, and the Garw Valley in Glamorgan is no exception. Passenger trains disappeared as long ago as 1953, but there is still plenty of coal traffic to Bridgend and the Margam marshalling yard on the outskirts of Port Talbot. Cardiff Canton's 37257, fitted with twin tanks for extra range, had charge of the Tondu-Blaengarw coal empties through Pontycymmer on the afternoon of 13 May 1983. Delivered from Vulcan Foundry as D6957, the loco has been on these sort of duties continuously since January 1965.
(Mrs D A Robinson)
Pentax 6 × 7   Ektachrome 200   1/500, f6.3

Overleaf
The presence of 37s at Westbury for the considerable Mendip stone traffic leads to their use on other, less onerous duties in the area. The surviving section of the former Cheddar Valley line which forms the tiny Somerset branch from Witham to Cranmore makes up for its length by generating a staggering amount of traffic for BR, thanks to the Foster Yeoman Merehead stone terminal along its route. There is also a little bitumen traffic to the Anglo-American asphalt depot at Cranmore, also home of the East Somerset Railway preservation group. Since this view of 37290 was taken shunting empty tanks on 2 February 1983, this hitherto exclusively Cardiff or Landore loco (D6990, built July 1965), has been refurbished as 37411 for Scotland.
(Michael Mensing)
Bronica S2A   75mm Nikkor
Agfachrome R100S (rated 160ASA)
1/250, f8

A summer Saturday morning at Castle Cary not long before the elimination of semaphore signalling, and 37306 has strayed from its traditional South Wales haunts to work a local ballast train. This is one of the final series (it was delivered new to Landore in October 1965) that was overhauled just before the eth conversion programme started, and thus remains a loco with its maintenance bills paid by the Railfreight sector. 28 July 1984.

(Michael Mensing)
Bronica S2A Nikkor 75mm
Agfachrome R100S 1/1000, f5

A Mark 1 barrier coach has had to be provided to enable 37276 to haul a dead HST set 253015 (minus front power car) through Patchway on the outskirts of Bristol on 23 March 1980, perhaps on its way for repair at St. Philip's Marsh depot. Transfer away of much of the WR's spare motive power now sees South Wales 37s on such diverse duties as vans to London, Lickey bankers, summer Saturday trips on the Cambrian, and the inevitable stone trains. 37276 isn't around on the WR anymore, having been transferred to Scotland via Crewe Works for refurbishment, eth fitment and renumbering as 37413. *(Geoff Cann)*
Pentax MX   50mm   Kodachrome 64
1/250, f5.6

Cardiff and Landore once maintained a fleet of 18 boiler-fitted Class 37s, Nos 37175-92, for services such as those in West Wales, but displacement by 33s and 47s from 1981 onwards saw them scattered far and wide. Some changed allegiance to Scotland (37188 is now named *Jimmy Shand*!), while others had their heating equipment isolated and stayed in South Wales for ordinary freight use. One such loco is 37189, and this view of the old way of things shows it passing Fishguard and Goodwick station and signalbox on a passenger working from Swansea on the afternoon on 12 April 1982. Shunter in the yard is 08649. (*Andrew Marshall*)
Minolta SRT 100X 45mm Rokkor Kodachrome 64 1/250, f8

Left. The shape of things to come. 37196 certainly stood out in a crowd after it was repainted at St Blazey depot in Railfreight livery for exhibition at depot open days to celebrate the 150th anniversary of the Great Western Railway. Named *Tre Pol and Pen* after the Cornish legend, it became a regular sight on china clay duties as this 6 September view shows. The processing plant at Burngullow towers over 37196 and last-built 37308, and the pride of train crews is shown by the locomotive headboard. *(John S Whiteley)*
Pentax SP Kodachrome 25 1/250, f4

Above. A pair of Lizzards... China clay workings in the south-west are now almost totally handled by pairs of Laira-based Class 37 locomotives, although as can be seen, the wagons this pair was towing into Lostwithiel on 22 August 1985 were certainly overdue for renewal. A brief flurry of local patriotism and independence saw the locos' BR 'barbed wire' logos on their bodysides replaced by Cornish lizzards, and 37181 and 37207 looked the smarter for it. The former is one of the last to retain its black headcode marker lights and was one of the machines involved in the 1965 WR high-speed trials. No 37207 was named *William Cookworthy* after the china clay pioneer at St Austell station in May 1982. *(John S Whiteley)*
Pentax SP 85mm Takumar
Kodachrome 25 1/250, f3.5

27

How we will miss that imposing GWR signal bracket that guarded the southern end of Exeter St David's for countless years, and has now swept away by the West of England MAS scheme! The loco passing under it is split headcode 37096, distinctly off its beaten track with the 1Z31 1030 York-Plymouth relief on 9 August 1984. Apart from crew-training, the early series of 37s were never allocated to the WR, although refurbishing as Railfreight Class 37/5s would see this change from 1986 onwards. 37096, new in November 1962, lost its boiler early on. *(Hugh Dady)*
Nikkormat FT2   50mm Nikkor
Kodachrome 64   1/500, f3.5

It was good news indeed when increased track maintenance meant the lifting of the ban that prevailled in the early 1980s on loco-hauled services on the Central Wales Line. Nos 37233 and 37247 were rostered for a SLOA 'Welsh Marches Express', diverted and diesel-hauled due to a high fire risk on 12 May 1984. The train is seen passing through the magnificent Welsh borderland countryside at Stowe, east of Knighton. *(Geoffrey F Bannister)*
Olympus OM1-N   85mm Zuiko
Kodachrome 64   1/250, f5.6

Right. South Yorkshire remains traditional Class 37 territory, with a substantial allocation at Tinsley and frequent visits from units based at other ER depots like Immingham and Thornaby. A proverbial sea of merry-go-round HAA coal wagons as far as the eye can see was the scene in the yards south of Doncaster on 4 January 1984, and 37161's own train added a few more to the South Yorkshire collection. Don't be deceived into thinking this is a scene of decline however – many of the hoppers will only be standing literally for a few minutes before moving on the colliery/power station circuit. Twin-tank fitted for extra range, 37161 started life on the WR as D6861 in mid-1963, but was transferred to Hull Dairycoates in 1966 as a direct replacement for steam locomotives such as WD 2-8-0s. It has been a familiar local feature ever since. *(John S Whiteley)*
Pentax 6 × 7
150mm Takumar
Ektachrome 200
1/500, f6.3

Opposite. A typical day's work for non-boilered 37065, passing Sunderland South Dock with coal empties from Seaham on 27 July 1983. It was delivered new to Thornaby in November 1962, and has barely been away from the North-East ever since. *(Peter J Robinson)*
Pentax 6 × 7
Ektachrome 200
1/250, f6.3

Above. 37082 and its train of coal empties bring some life to a barren landscape in August 1982. The double-track line to the Steetley building materials plant in the distance is one of the handful on the BR system that doesn't even close on Christmas day. Although many still mourn the passing of steam in the North-East, few can argue that a Class 37 isn't photogenic. *(John S Whiteley)*

Olympus OM1   85mm Zuiko
Kodachrome 64   1/250, f6.3

Right. Diesel-electric meets diesel-hydraulic. Ashington stills retains a complex rail network as the centre of activity of traffic serving the Northumberland coalfields, but not for much longer, we feel. Steam was completely supplanted by 1967, and Class 37s were largely to blame. Originally delivered to Sheffield Tinsley, 37053 lost its steam-heat equipment (and its nose-end doors) at an early stage, and spent the years 1974-81 at Gateshead and Thornaby. Here it leaves Ashington Colliery with coal for Blyth power station, passing former BR Class 14 0-6-0 No 506 (D9504). The date, 1 October 1980. *(Mrs D A Robinson)*
Pentax 6 × 7   Ektachrome 200   1/500, f5.6

The ER's allocation of 119 Class 37s between 1960-63 was supplemented after two years by a further ten of the centre headcode variety, D6959-68. Delivered to Tinsley in the first instance, they later migrated to the Great Eastern before the mass movements of the mid-1970s saw them scattered far and wide. The first of them, now 37259, was the only one anywhere near its original home by late 1985, based at Thornaby. On 11 May 1982 it was heading south over Durham viaduct with a mixed freight. *(Paul Shannon)*
Olympus OM1   Zoom at 100mm
Kodachrome 64   1/250, f5.6-8

There's no mistaking where this shot was taken – a none-too-clean Class 37 pauses at Berwick with its southbound chemicals train well insulated by barrier wagons on 4 August 1981, waiting for an HST to pass. 37125 has had divided loyalty since being delivered new to Cardiff in May 1983, and has demonstrated the usefulness of the class by transfer as required to such diverse locations as Hull, Gateshead, Stratford, March, Tinsley, Immingham, Stratford, and at the end of 1985 off to Motherwell. *(Les Nixon)*
Pentax 6 × 7 150mm Takumar
Ektachrome 200

Right. A chilly winter's day in the North-East, and 37078 goes about its usual work, the same old coal empties through Blyth Cambois from the nearby power station to Low Fell sidings. Gateshead and Thornaby have shared the use of this loco since it was brand new as D6778 back in October 1962. This shot is dated 19 February 1978. *(Mrs D A Robinson)* Pentax 6 × 7 Ektachrome 200 1/500, f8

Opposite. The time-honoured Harwich-North West through train has undergone many changes of route over the years. Now known as the Glasgow/Edinburgh-Harwich "European", it was the Harwich-Manchester when this snow scene was captured on 17 December 1969. The location is Bullhouse on the much-lamented 1500V dc Manchester-Sheffield/Wath line through Woodhead tunnel. Loco is green-liveried D6960, now exiled in Scotland on the Far North Line as 37260 *Radio Highland*. *(Les Nixon)* Leica M2 50mm Summilux Kodachrome II 1/250, f3.5

Right. The already notable career of 37268 was carried through to 1984 when it was chosen as the first to undergo refurbishment and conversion to electric-heat 37401 for Scotland. As D6968, it was the last of a series of ten with boilers delivered to the Eastern Region in February 1965, was later borrowed by the Derby Railway Technical Centre for air-brake tests, and spent the years 1977-84 in the Western Region's South Wales pool. Latest honour is the attachment of *Mary Queen of Scots* nameplates at Linlithgow (her birthplace) on 4 November 1985. This view shows 37268 in its unconverted state at Crewe Holding Sidings on 5 April 1980. *(Barry J Nicolle)*
Olympus OM1   Agfa CT18   1/250, f5.6

Left. The revamped Class 37 that will be with us into the 21st century – pristine ex-works 37404, 37403 and 37401 stand in Basford Hall Yard, Crewe on 28 June 1985, having just been released from Crewe Works for the first time that afternoon and all destined for Scotland. Prior to refurbishment, which included replacing the main generator with an alternator, installing eth equipment, fitting new wheelsets, extensive rewiring and cab modernisation, the locomotives were (in order stated) 37286 (ex-Cardiff), 37307 (ex-Landore) and 37268 (ex-Landore). Early repaints were with hand-painted bodyside numbers, and all have since been named – 37404 *Ben Cruachan*, 37403 *Isle of Mull* and 37401 *Mary Queen of Scots*.
(David Rapson)
Canon AE1   50mm
Kodachrome 64   1/125, f8

It was a major blow to BREL Doncaster Works to lose the Class 37 repair and overhaul contract in 1982 after 20 years of continuous maintenance of the 300-odd members of the class. Doncaster turned to Class 31s and 50s while Crewe took over the EE Type 3s and in 1984 picked up the refurbishment programme as well. This was the scene in the Doncaster Crimpsall Shops on 17 June 1978 when 37266 (nearest the camera) was undergoing attention. It is now 37422. Also in the frame are, from left, 37072, Brush 31286, Deltic 55008 *The Green Howards* and 37141. *(Hugh Dady)* *Praktica IV   28mm Vivitar* *Kodachrome 64   1/10, f9*

Left. The Scottish region did not receive any 37s new, though small numbers surplus to WR requirements soon found their way north. This process accelerated in the early 1980s as the ScR sought to replace its Sulzer-engined Bo-Bos on the West Highland and Highland/Far North lines. The Region's desire for domestic autonomy prompted unscheduled depot re-paints for large numbers of steam-heat Class 37s transferred in from the Great Eastern and South Wales, especially if a naming ceremony had been laid on, and the out-dated plain blue was replaced by this – extended wrap-around yellow ends, black cab-window surrounds, large bodyside BR logo, and extra-large numbers. 37191, with extra embellishments of black headcode panels and snowploughs, stands at Eastfield TMD on 17 February 1985 with former Class 25 pre-heat unit 97250 *(ETHEL 1)*. It was named *International Youth Year 1985* at Glasgow Queen Street on 21 January and as the name suggests only carried the plates until the end of year. *(Tom Noble)*
Mamiya 645   Ektachrome 200   1/200, f8

Right. Displaced steam-heat Class 37s were transferred to Inverness in May 1982 to replace Birmingham Class 26s and to speed up services on the Far North and Kyle of Lochalsh routes. This however is something special – the stock of an excursion from Wellingborough is double-headed along the edge of Loch Carron at Strome Ferry as the strengthened 1055 Inverness-Kyle. Locos are 37114 and 37183, and the date 28 April 1984. 37114, since named *Dunrobin Castle*, started life at Tinsley in February 1963. 37183 by contrast was a West Wales passenger loco for the best part of a decade. *(Mrs D A Robinson)*
Pentax 6 × 7   Ektachrome 200   1/500, f6.3

Not an easy task even for a pair of Class 37s – 37188 and 37149 face up to the climb to Crianlarich from Glenfallock on 1 May 1984 with the 0520 Mossend-Mallaig Junction (Fort William) ABS. These interesting partners have gone their separate ways since – 37188 was named *Jimmy Shand* after the Scottish entertainer at Oban the following year, while 37149 returned to its original South Wales habitat after a 19-year break.

(Bob Osborne)
Canon AE1 50mm Kodachrome 64
1/500, f4

Corrour is West Scotland's loneliest station – there isn't even a road to it. A lonely 37111 only had one ballast wagon in its charge as it headed south on 8 August 1981. The loco was one of three (the others were 37027 and 37112) given wrap-around yellow ends at Eastfield depot in 1981, and later returned to their original colours. They retained their distinguishing central bodyside numbers for some time afterwards. *(Paul Shannon)*
Olympus OM1   50mm Zuiko
Kodachrome 64   1/250, f5.6

Right. From the flat landscapes of eastern England to the majestic grandeur of Scotland's West Highland line – that was the move made in 1981 by 1961-built 37012. The name *Loch Rannoch*, bestowed at Fort William on 31 March 1982, revived that carried by one of the Gresley K2 2-6-0s which characterised the West Highland for many years. Kinloid, near Arisaig, is the setting for this study of 37012 heading the 1245 Mallaig-Glasgow Queen Street on 21 June 1982. *(Mrs D A Robinson)*
Pentax 6 × 7   Ektachrome 200   1/500, f6.3-8

Opposite. Full marks to ScotRail for improvisation. Air-conditioned stock was transferred into Scottish domestic services before Class 37s could be converted from steam to electric heat, and three redundant Class 25s were modified in 1983 as mobile generator units as a stopgap measure. The Euston-Fort William 'Royal Highlander' is thus upgraded on 24 April 1984, with Eastfield's oldest Class 37 loco No 37011 and 97251 (nicknamed *ETHEL 2*) at the head, speeding through Torlundy. Starting life as D6711 at Stratford in March 1961, 37011 was sent to Scotland almost exactly 20 years later. *(Mrs D A Robinson)*
Pentax 6 × 7   Ektachrome 200   1/1000, f5.6

One of the hardest tasks currently entrusted to pairs of Class 37s must be the iron ore trains between Hunterston and Ravenscraig, and although this is nominally a Motherwell duty, locos from other depots frequently join in. Approaching Ardrossan from the north on 27 April 1984 were 'white stripe' 37012 *Loch Rannoch* and 37144 both borrowed from Eastfield. The former, boiler-fitted, is more used to passenger workings on the West Highland Line, and owes its name to a rather less than ambitious competition run by the Scottish Region in March 1982. It started life working from Stratford in 1961. 37144 was a Cardiff loco from 1963 to 1966. *(Les Nixon)*
Pentax 6 × 7 150mm Takumar
Ektachrome 200 1/500, f5.6

In these days of unbridled livery experimentation, it is worth recalling the furore that Eastfield's unofficial application of a white stripe to the lower bodysides of their Class 37 fleet caused. (One, No 37196, was painted with a red stripe). People in high places demanded their instant removal. Still, those were the days of all-over blue. 37111, complete with offending stripe when photographed on freight at Dundee on 17 May 1984, was the victim of an earlier painting experiment (wrap-round yellow ends), and got the now standard passenger livery with large bodyside BR logo and large numbers at Eastfield prior to its naming as *Loch Eil Outward Bound* on 20 April 1985. *(Hugh Dady)*
Nikkormat FT2 50mm Nikkor
Kodachrome 64 1/250, f5.6

Left. Newly-delivered PKAs head a long rake of empty car-carrying vehicles to show up a rather scruffy 37045 on its early evening departure from Millerhill yard, Edinburgh on 14 June 1982. Unlike many of the early series of 37s, the then D6745 migrated from Great Eastern territory as early as 1970, lost its boiler and has been a North Eastern-based loco ever since. *(Mrs D A Robinson)*
Pentax 6 × 7   Ektachrome 200   1/500, f6.3

Above. More than a slight colour clash at Stranraer on 26 May 1985 as wanderlust 37024 of Tinsley arrives with the 1505 service from Glasgow. The stock comprises conventional Mark 1 vehicles in colours chosen by Sealink (you have to blame someone!). The loco, brand new to March in August 1961, has long lost its heating equipment, but in May no-one would really notice. *(Rodney A Lissenden)*
Pentax 6 × 7   Agfa RS100   1/250, f8

49

Polmadie's D6841 had still not been defaced with a full yellow end as late as 25 November 1970, as this late view of the lost and lamented Carstairs signal gantry proves. And as the headcode shows, this is the 8S53 Carlisle-Ravenscraig freight. The loco returned to its original Cardiff base at the end of 1972, but after two years found a new home, this time on the Eastern. *(Derek Cross)*
Rolliflex 66   Zeiss Planar 80mm
Agfa CT18 Professional

There was a great deal more activity at Chinley Junction when this vintage view of Tinsley's five-year-old D6751 was captured by the camera with a Manchester-Sheffield freight on 11 May 1967. This loco spent many years at March before the mass exodus to Scotland in 1981, but unlike many of its colleagues was not rewarded with a nameplate. *(Derek Cross)*
Linhof Technika Zeiss 100mm
Agfa CT18 Professional

Left. Penetrating deep into the Pennines, the freight-only single track branch from Bishop Auckland serves the cement works at Eastgate, and a good deal of patience is required to get any photograph at all. 37172 was a March loco when it was in charge of the westbound empties through Frosterley, just short of its destination, on 12 March 1982. Since new as D6872 to Landore in 1965, the loco has worked from a variety of Eastern, North Eastern and Scottish depots before returning to South Wales in March 1985. *(Les Nixon)*
Nikon F   85mm Nikkor
Kodachrome 25   1/250, f3.8

Above. The Clitheroe-Gunnie (Coatbridge) clinker/cement is one of the most familiar freights on the West Coast Main Line, not least because it runs in daylight and is operated by double-headed Class 37s instead of electric motive power. It was the turn of 37172 and 37150 to negotiate Shap summit on 5 July 1984, seen here at Greenholme. The former was new to Cardiff in 1963, and has strayed to such diverse depots as Gateshead, Immingham and March before returning to Cardiff. 37150, the former D6850, was a Scottish loco for two decades before moving to Cardiff as well.
(Gavin Morrison)
Pentax SP1000   Kodachrome 64   1/500, f4.5

The test train explains why March depot's 37173 was so far from home on 12 April 1984, having brought the High Speed Track recording coach and two other vehicles to Liverpool Lime Street from Newcastle. The later centre-headcode 37s seem to flit from one depot to another almost by the month, but the former D6873 (new to Cardiff in September 1963) has been more docile and has only moved five times in all. *(David Rapson)*

Canon AE1 50mm Agfa CT18 1/60, f4

The new order on Peak Forest stone trains in the 1980s was pairs of Class 37s, progressively replacing their exhausted older Class 40 sisters. This view shows the old and new order together – 40150 stands at signals and 37128 and 37086 reverse in. The former 37 was built new for Cardiff in 1965, the latter for Gateshead in 1962. The date, 11 August 1983.

(John S Whiteley)
Olympus OM1   85mm Zuiko
Kodachrome 64   1/250, f6.3

Right. There really is life after the Class 40s! Removal of the headcode boxes on a handful of collision damaged Class 37s gives a distinct feeling of *déjà vu* as 37006 negotiates the climb at Armathwaite in a rare sortie on the Settle and Carlisle line on 21 August 1984. The train is a Carlisle-Appleby freight and the locomotive a vintage machine that as D6706 was delivered new to Norwich depot for crew training in January 1961. Heavy general repairs on these locomotives from late 1985 made headcode box removal statutory.
(Les Nixon)
Nikon F
85mm Nikkor
Kodachrome 25
1/250, f8

Opposite. The pair of gas holders towering over the railway fill the camera frame at Ravenhead Junction, St Helens. 37169 is in charge of the Cowley Hill-Stanlow oil train on 26 April 1984, demonstrating the more frequent appearances by the class in the North-West following the rundown of the 40s and 25s. Delivered new to Landore in August 1963, the former D6869 migrated to Healey Mills in 1966 and stayed in the area ever since. *(Kim Fullbrook)*
Canon 35-70mm Zoom
Kodachrome 64
1/250, f5.6

Left. Goose Hill Junction between Normanton and Wakefield is where the L&Y to Manchester (passenger) and Midland to Sheffield (now freight only) routes divide. It was also the place to see split-headcode 37029 on 23 May 1983, complete with rake of coal empties. The loco, new to Stratford in 1961, has long lost its boiler, and on dual-brake conversion in 1978 was transferred to Gateshead. It was part of the Tinsley stable at the end of 1985.
(Rodney A Lissenden)
Pentax 6 × 7
Ektachrome 200
150m Takumar
1/500, f6.3

Right. Its glory days seemingly over, the pioneer D6700 traverses the now-axed Manchester southern avoiding route from Skelton Junction to Warrington on 18 January 1984 with the 6F45 Ashburys-Arpley air-braked freight. Delivered from Vulcan Foundry to Stratford in December 1960, this loco's achievements include selection for push-pull trials between Edinburgh and Glasgow in early 1968. The TOPS renumbering scheme (and the computer's inability to cope with a loco 37000) saw D6700 amended to 37119 as the last of the split headcode series. Loco 6819 should have taken the number 37119 but instead became 37283, using the gap left by the write-off of D6983 in the Bridgend accident of December 1965 to allow the prototype to remain within its split-box series.
(Bob Osborne)
Canon AE1   100mm
Kodachrome 64   1/250, f4

Left. Most trains go through Tinsley yard without stopping nowadays – the declining importance of this modern Sheffield marshalling yard is obvious in this 31 May 1985 scene where, apart from a passing mgr working, most activity seems to be centred on lifting redundant trackwork. (The mgr's hoppers are empty at that!) Locos at the front are Tinsley pair 37075 and 37064, the latter with a home-grown livery modification of white window frames and numbers both ends, a thoroughly short-lived effort. The leading locomotive clearly demonstrates the interim front-end tidy up carried out at Doncaster in the late-1970s, where an overhaul has included sealing up the useless connecting doors, to the relief of crews chilled to the bone by winter draughts made more acute at 80mph. *(Ian Gould)*
Pentax 6 × 7   200mm Takumar
Agfachrome RS100   1/250, f8

Above. 37201 has about as many horsepower as all these new Ford cars put together as it approaches Normanton from the north on 29 June 1983. This busy Yorkshire junction still has a four-track layout – but for how long we wonder? Although it started its career in 1963 working from Cardiff Canton, 37201 has been based on the other side of the country since 1967, most recently at Immingham.
(John S Whiteley)
Pentax 6 × 7   Ektachrome 200   1/500, f6.3

An interesting aspect of Class 37 operation almost from the beginning has been their use on summer Saturday dated passenger turns to holiday destinations, often offering the chance of freight power haulage over lines usually worked by dmus. Few locations have changed less in 140 years than the remote East Lincolnshire outpost of Havenhouse on the Grantham-Skegness line. Even the GN somersault signals are original, and the only features spoiling the view are unsympathetic steel lamp-posts on the platforms and 1970s 'modern image' signs. This is another view of 37259, storming through with the 0710 Sheffield-Skegness on 16 June 1984.
(David Stacey)
Pentax KX Kodachrome 25 1/250, f4

A brief interlude of freight Class 37s on summer Saturday workings to the Cambrian coast was a 1985 stop-gap between life-expired BR/Sulzer Class 25s and the refurbished Class 37/4s that would enable air-conditioned stock to be used from the start of the 1986 season. Taken straight out of the Cardiff freight pool, 37163 and 37176 power the 0730 Euston-Aberystwyth across the trestle bridge over the Afon Clettwr between Dovey Junction and Borth on 27 July 1985. Darlington-built 37163 spent 18 years in the North-East sandwiched between South Wales work, but Vulcan's 37176 has not been the greatest of travellers. *(Mike Robinson)*
Pentax ME Super
50mm SMC Takumar   Kodachrome 64
1/500, f4

Class 37s broke one of their last patches of new ground from the summer of 1985 when the North Wales Coast line was chosen for running ex-works Class 37/4s on test from Crewe Works after rebuilding. Its paintwork still glistening, 37405 (the former 37282) speeds through Llysfaen near Colwyn Bay on 30 August. Its 20 years on miscellaneous South Wales freight jobs have gone for ever, and a new career beckons as a fully-fledged passenger loco. *(Larry Goddard)*
Pentax SP1000   105mm Takumar
Ektachrome 100   1/250, f8